The KidHaven Science Library

Maps

by Wendy Lanier

KIDHAVEN PRESS

An imprint of Thomson Gale, a part of The Thomson Corporation

THOMSON
™
GALE

Detroit • New York • San Francisco • New Haven, Conn. • Waterville, Maine • London

LIBRARY OF CONGRESS CATALOGING-IN-PUBLICATION DATA

Lanier, Wendy, 1963–
   Maps / by Wendy Lanier.
     p. cm. — (Kidhaven science library)
  Includes bibliographical references and index.
    ISBN-13: 978-0-7377-3632-8 (hardcover)
   1. Cartography—Juvenile literature. I. Title.
GA105.6.L37 2007
912–dc22

2007024356

ISBN-10: 0-7377-3632-1

Printed in the United States of America

Contents

Chapter 1

Early Maps and How They Were Made

The first maps were drawn to help show places that could not be easily seen by other people. Even before there were other forms of written communication, maps were drawn as a way to show the places they had visited. Sometimes the maps were drawn on the ground with a stick. A few were drawn on rocks or cave walls.

These first maps were based on the natural features of the land, like a river, a group of trees, or a big rock. The features could and did change over time. Even if the map didn't change, the land it was supposed to show often did because of weather, fire, or other natural events.

As man began to explore farther and farther from home, his need for maps grew. It was important to know where he wanted to go and what to expect when he got there. Maps also showed where not to go and how to avoid hostile people or dangerous land.

The earliest surviving maps still in existence are these Babylonian clay tablets that date from about 2500 B.C..

Babylonian Clay Tablets

The earliest maps still in existence are Babylonian clay tablets. Experts can't seem to agree on exactly how old they are, but most authorities date them at about 2500 B.C. The tablets are artifacts from the Babylonian empire, which was located in what is now Iraq.

One of the tablets, about the size of the palm of your hand, shows a river running between two hilly areas. The hills are marked with overlapping semicircles and a line marks the path of the river. Cities are shown with circles. Other identifying marks are the names of some of the cities, the identity of the owner of a plot of land, and the **cardinal directions**.

Egyptian Maps

Unlike the Babylonians, the ancient Egyptians were more interested in developing their own form of writing than in making maps. But each year the flooding of the Nile River made it necessary to reestablish the boundaries of private property. The Egyptians used their knowledge of geometry to **survey** the land and calculate the property lines. They drew maps on papyrus (a type of paper).

One papyrus map dating to about 1300 B.C. shows the Nile River with mountains to the east where gold and silver were mined at that time. Also shown are the locations of wells, shelters for the miners, and a network of roads in the described area. The map is especially interesting because of the mapmaker's precise drawing, use of color, and inscriptions.

Early Chinese Maps

During the time of the Egyptian and Babylonian mapmaking progress, the people of Far Eastern countries, such as China, were making great strides in developing their own mapmaking skills. Chinese **cartographers**, or people who draw maps, were creating more detailed and more accurate maps than many others of the same time. A recent find in a Han Dynasty tomb in China revealed two maps, one a military map and the other **topographical**. Predated by only the Babylonian clay tablets, the maps show a consistent use of **scale** and advanced symbols, and they are reasonably correct in content. Both portray roads, settlements, and landscape in the southern Hu-nan Province of China. The military map includes military plans and color. Both maps reveal a level of mapmaking skill far advanced of those in other areas.

Ancient Greek Maps

Like the Chinese, the ancient Greeks were known for their discoveries and innovations. Hundreds of years before explorer Christopher Columbus made his famous voyage proving the Earth was round, Greek philosophers already understood this concept. By 200 B.C., a Greek mathematician named Eratosthenes may have correctly calculated the distance around the Earth. Famous even in his own time, Eratosthenes used his knowledge of mathematics and angles to calculate the Earth's **circumference** as 250,000 stadia. Depending on the accepted definition of stadia, this measurement may be very close to the actual distance of 25,000 miles (46,000 km).

Greek scholar Ptolemy wrote what would be considered the world's first atlas.

About 350 years later, another Greek scholar named Ptolemy built on Eratosthenes' work to write a series of eight books. Today the books would be considered an atlas. In them he defined the basic principles of **cartography** and laid the foundation for modern mapmaking. Although not completely accurate, the books contained the first world map and proposed a system of **projections** for creating flat maps to represent the Earth and a grid system for locating places and geographical features on a globe. The grid lines became known as lines of **latitude** and **longitude** and are still being used today.

Maps of the Middle Ages

From about A.D. 400 to the 1400s, the Chinese and Arab worlds continued to improve their cartography skills as the Greek Empire (and later, the Roman) came to an end. During this time, known as the Middle Ages, mapmaking in Europe became more of an art form than true illustrations of actual places. Maps were based on the reports of travelers and explorers and drawn by someone who had never seen the described locations. Mapmakers often guessed at the things they weren't sure about and filled in any blank spaces with imaginative drawings. The drawings were influenced by religious beliefs or the mapmaker's own special interest.

Mapmaking Progress

By the start of the 15th century, the Middle Ages (sometimes called the Dark Ages) were coming to an end. The new Age of Discovery, or Renaissance, brought a renewed desire for knowledge and information. At the same time, the invention of the printing press was making it possible to produce large numbers of the same map for wider distribution. These maps became greatly valued for their help with commerce, travel, and military operations.

The world maps used in classrooms today are similar to the one created by cartographer Gerardus Mercator in 1569.

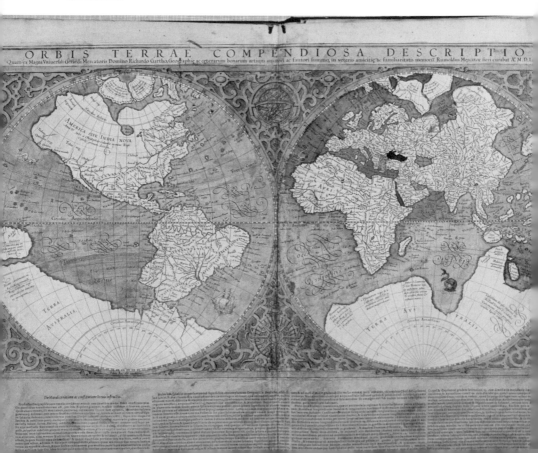

As explorers of the 16th century began returning from world voyages, the need for accurate world maps became great. In 1569, a leading cartographer named Gerardus Mercator published a map of the world based on his newly developed **cylindrical projection**. The result was a world map resembling the ones often used in today's classrooms. In spite of other projections soon to follow, Mercator's remains the most widely used for navigation charts and world maps today.

19th Century Cartography

Over the next two centuries, cartographers continued to make steady improvements. By the 19th century, some of the most accurate maps were being made by surveyors. Surveyors were people who traveled around the countryside gathering information for drawing maps. They studied the countryside, made notes about the physical features of the land, and took measurements. In 1824, two famous surveyors, Meriwether Lewis and William Clark, took on the task of mapping unexplored portions of North America.

Using instruments called theodolites, Lewis and Clark gathered compass readings and measured distances. A theodolite is an instrument consisting of a small telescope and a level mounted on a tripod. By calculating distances and observing angles, they drew out series of triangles that accurately mapped the areas they visited. This method of mapping is called triangulation.

Other tools of the surveying trade at this time included telescopes, compasses, and sextants. Telescopes were, of course, the first forms of binoculars used for seeing objects at a distance. Sextants were instruments composed of a telescope attached to a device used to measure angles. Surveyors took measurements of the angle of a star from a point on the Earth. The angle and the time of measurement were used to calculate a position on a chart.

As the 20th century drew near, maps had become increasingly reliable tools. The general size and shape of the Earth had been established, as well as the location of the major continents. There were fairly accurate maps of most places, especially those with the greatest populations. Maps had proven to be useful in travel, business, diplomacy, and war. Creating accurate maps had been the life's work of many cartographers. It would, however, be left to the scientists of the 20th century to discover ways to map the unknown and less-populated regions of the world.

Chapter 2

Twentieth-Century Maps

The 20th century brought enormous changes in the way maps were made, as well as the kinds of information they contained. Mapmaking became less an art form and more pure science. Theodolites, telescopes, and sextants gave way to electronic measuring devices, computers, global positioning satellites, and other technology. The maps the new technology created showed more than just the shape of the land. They became tools for displaying various kinds of other information, such as population density, political climate, and weather patterns.

Aerial Photography

One of the first breakthroughs of the 20th century came with the invention of the airplane in 1903. Within a few years, it became possible to photograph hard-to-reach places from the air. Aerial photography, a type of remote sensing, allowed for the construction of maps with photographs taken from the air. This technology came just in time for military use in World War I.

Remote sensing is a way of observing an object or place without actually being there. It uses instruments, usually aboard aircraft or spacecraft, to collect and record data. The devices used for gathering the data have progressed from simple cameras to technologically advanced satellites and space probes. Other types of remote-sensing devices allow scientists to "see" underwater and underground.

Sonar

In 1912, the ship thought to be "unsinkable," the *Titanic*, sank in the North Atlantic. Not long afterward, World War I began. Technology developed an ocean-going ship known as the submarine. This became the newest weapon of war. Both the sinking of the *Titanic* and the introduction of the submarine gave scientists new reasons to map a place they could not see—the ocean floor. Sound navigation ranging, or sonar, another type of remote sensing, was developed to help scientists explore the depths of the ocean.

With sonar, scientists beamed high-pitched sounds, called ultrasound, underwater. These penetrating sound waves were released by the vibration of a crystal inside the sonar equipment, producing a sharp "ping." As the sound traveled

Maps of the ocean floor are partially created by the use of sonar.

underwater, its signal bounced off the ocean floor, or any objects in its path, causing an echo to travel back through the water to special listening devices. By measuring the time required for a signal to travel from a survey ship to the ocean floor and back, scientists were able to calculate the depth of the water. Repeated measurements over a long distance allowed them to "see" the shape of the ocean floor for the first time. It also allowed them to locate objects such as submarines lurking beneath the waves.

Through the use of sonar, scientists were surprised to discover there were mountains, hills, valleys, and plains on the ocean floor, just as there were on dry land. This led to the discovery of the **mid-Atlantic Ridge** and, eventually, to the theory of **plate tectonics**. For the first time, scientists were able to see the shape of the Earth's entire crust.

Radar

By the late 1940s, a technology similar to sonar was introduced. Radar, or radio detection and ranging, allowed for the mapping of areas from the air in spite of cloudy conditions or rain. Radar instruments carried aboard airplanes transmitted a narrowly beamed radio signal toward the ground. The reflected signal was then recorded by the instruments to reveal the shape of the landscape. Radar was a great improvement over aerial photography because it could be used day or night through all but extremely dense clouds and rain.

In the 1970s, radar was improved by the development of side-looking airborne radar (SLAR). With it scientists were able to create three-dimensional images of the Earth's surface. This led to the discovery of previously unmapped features of the land. It also allowed for the correction of errors in maps already made.

Satellites

While sonar and radar were being perfected, other technologies were coming into play as well. In 1957, the launch of the Russian satellite *Sputnik* marked the beginning of the space age and the race to the Moon. A few months later, in early 1958, a second satellite was launched by the United States. By the end of the century, there were more than 2,200 satellites orbiting the Earth. The new satellite technology proved to have many uses, although its most immediate impact would be on creating new and better maps.

Satellites were, and continue to be, valuable for their ability to see parts of the light spectrum not visible to the eye alone, such as infrared light and the thermal infrared given off by heat sources. They are also able to pick up radio frequencies, like shortwave, that are beyond the regular

Satellites have provided unique new ways to view the Earth, from tracking storms to showing land forms, as this image of the Iberian Peninsula shows.

broadcast band. This gives satellites the ability to "see" and "hear" things from high above the Earth.

Because of their special abilities, satellites are capable of gathering, storing, and sending back to Earth a variety of information. The Landsat satellites launched by NASA (National Aeronautics and Space Administration) in the 1970s sent back detailed data that could be made into colored pictures. The pictures and data provided by Landsat have been used to manage crops, find fault lines, track weather, and observe changes in the land and its use from year to year.

The First Computer Technology and Mapmaking

Landsat satellites, and satellites in general, were able to collect and send enormous amounts of information. The sheer volume of the information made the use of computers a necessity. Computer technology, first developed as part of nuclear weapons research in the late 1940s and 1950s, was making steady advances along with satellites during that time. By the early 1960s, computers had progressed enough to be used for mapping and other general purposes.

In 1967, the first computer application for cartography, called the Geographic Information

A man views a Geographic Information System map showing the crime statistics for his neighborhood.

System (GIS), was developed in Canada. GIS was a system of hardware, software, and data about existing geographical features used to create and print desired maps. The system allowed the mapmaker to pull data from a variety of sources, make changes when necessary, and process digital information into map form before creating the final product.

One important use of GIS allowed for the overlapping of data to view more than one map at the same time. This made it possible, for example, to see how the geographic features of the land affected the number of people living in an area by viewing both maps at once. In this overlapping of a geographic map with a population map, GIS technology made short work of what had once been a time-consuming and difficult task.

In addition, GIS had the ability to show how an area had changed over time. This meant that scientists could study the effects of drought on a particular region or identify wetlands in need of protection. This information was helpful in deciding where to build new roads or housing developments and what impact they might have on the environment when built.

By the end of the 20th century, and now into the 21st, GIS has become the leading technology for creating geographical maps. GIS-generated maps have hundreds of uses. They are, for example, often used in scientific investigations and are frequently seen in use on crime scene investigation shows on television. Emergency management teams use them to plan evacuation routes in the event of a natural disaster or to calculate emergency response times. Whatever its use, GIS has made it possible to process a massive amount of information in a wide variety of forms more efficiently than ever before.

Chapter 3

Types of Maps and Their Uses

Modern cartography has come a long way since the time when a map was made simply to describe a specific location. Today, maps can establish ownership, define boundaries and borders, compare numbers, locate **geologic formations**, show weather patterns—and the list goes on and on. With the use of GIS, the possibilities are almost endless.

Physical Maps

One of the most common types of map is a physical map. Physical maps show all the physical or **geographical features** of an area, such as rivers, mountains, lakes, plains, and valleys. The height above sea level, or elevation, of each feature is often shown by color. A **map key** explains the range of elevations for each color. In most cases, green is used for areas at or near sea level, while the highest regions are shown in brown. Water is always shown in blue.

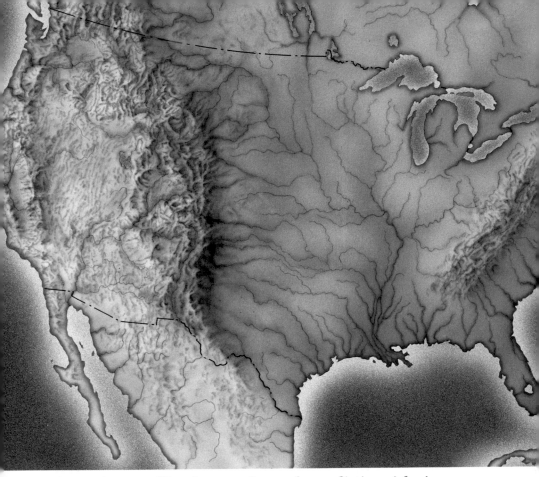

Physical maps, like the one shown here, distinguish rivers, mountains, plains, and other physical characteristics of the land.

Topographical Maps

Topographical maps are similar to physical maps in that they help describe the physical features of the land. However, topographical maps are primarily used to show elevation through the use of contour lines. Contour lines connect all the places that are the same distance above sea level. Each contour line is marked with a number. Any point along a given line has the same elevation. Lines that are close together indicate a steep slope. Lines drawn farther apart indicate a flat area or very gentle slope. Serious hikers like to have topographical maps to give them a better idea of how much climbing there will be in a planned hike.

Political Maps

A third common type of map is a political map. Political maps do not show physical features at all. Instead, they are used primarily to show boundaries and borders. A political map of the United States, for example, is designed to show the location and boundaries of all fifty states and the state capitals for each. The capitals are usually shown by a circle with a star in it.

Like a U.S. political map, a world political map shows the location and international borders of all the countries in the world along with their capitals. These types of political maps can and do change over time. Sometimes a country experiences a revolution or goes to war against an opposing country. When this happens, it is possible for a country to gain or lose territory. For this reason, old political maps may no longer be correct.

Political maps are useful for displaying all sorts of information not related to geography. For example, a political map might indicate which states have laws requiring motorcyclists to wear

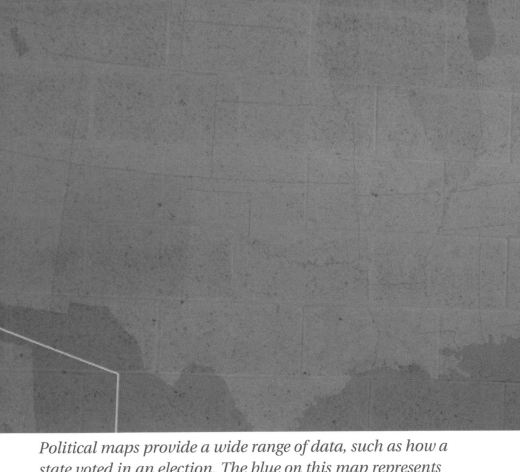

Political maps provide a wide range of data, such as how a state voted in an election. The blue on this map represents Democratic states and the red, Republican states.

helmets or how a state voted in the last election. Another political map may use color and shading to show **population density** in each state or country. At other times, maps might show historical data such as which countries fought together as a group in a war or where famous battles were fought. Maps used in this way allow readers to gather a lot of information at a glance.

Geological Maps

Maps showing the kinds and ages of rock lying beneath the surface of the Earth are called geological maps. Geologists, or scientists who study rocks, have known for a long time that certain types of rock and geologic formations are related to certain kinds of mineral deposits. Geological maps are useful for finding and exploring these natural resources and are of interest to scientists in a variety of fields.

Engineers use geological maps to locate construction materials and to predict foundation and excavation conditions. Hydrologists, or people who study water, use them to find underground water. Soil scientists, who specialize in the study of soils, use geological maps to classify different soils. In this way, they can determine which crops are best suited to be grown in a particular region.

Seismic Maps

Another type of map with special interest for geologists is a seismic map. Seismic mapping uses sound waves generated at the surface by small explosions or vibrations that penetrate the ground. Part of the wave is reflected back to the surface. There the speed, and strength of the wave is heard and timed by listening devices.

The information is analyzed to produce a map showing cross sections of the Earth's crust down to several thousand meters. This allows geologists to make better judgments about where oil and gas might be and to find evidence of faults, salt domes, or upward bulges of underground rock. This type of mapping can be done on land or offshore.

Weather Maps

An especially useful kind of map is a weather map. These types of maps show whole regions or an entire country. They have special symbols to show cold fronts and warm fronts, areas of high or low air pressure, and areas of **precipitation** or sunshine. Weather maps are commonly included in newspapers and shown on television news programs. They include information about current temperatures and what changes are due in the near future. By using a weather map, people can get a good idea of what the weather will be like for several days at a time.

Road Maps

Road maps are a type of map that makes getting from place to place much easier. State highway maps, city maps, bus route maps, and subway maps are all examples of road maps. Their purpose

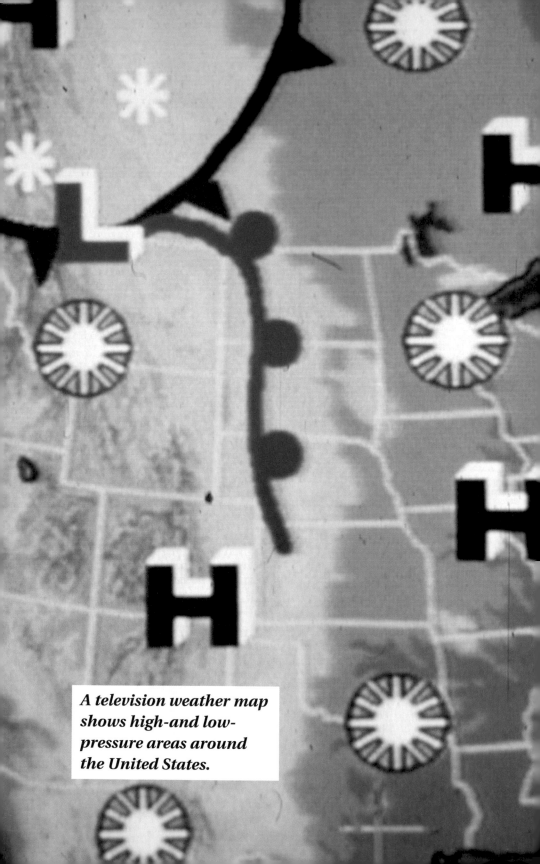

A television weather map shows high-and low-pressure areas around the United States.

is to help travelers find the places they want to go, whether the place is across the country, across the state, or just across town.

A state highway map is one kind of road map with information about roads and highways all across a state. The major roads and highways have names as well as numbers. Highway maps also include information about state parks, camping, roadside parks, airports, rest areas, information centers, and points of interest. Anyone traveling across state by car would find a state highway map a great help in locating the city they wish to visit.

While a state highway map may help a traveler reach a certain city, it won't be much help once they arrive there. Highway maps do not show individual cities in much detail. This is why it is necessary to have a city map to find locations within a particular city.

City Maps

City maps give large amounts of information about much smaller areas of land than highway maps do. They show railroads, water features, parks, recreational facilities, neighborhoods, cemeteries, public buildings, schools and universities, bus or trolley lines, military bases, and airports within a city, as well as streets. Visitors can use a city map to find the location of a zoo, an amusement park, or some other point of interest.

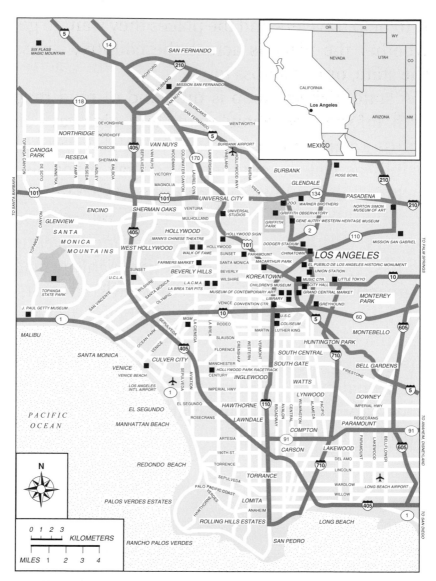

City maps, like this one of Los Angeles, California, give more detailed information about a smaller area of land.

Once a visitor locates the place within a city they wish to go, they may need to consult a transportation map to find a way to get there. Transportation maps are usually city maps with color-coded lines to show bus routes, trolley lines, or subway lines. The lines show where the type of transportation runs within the city and where it makes stops. Often the less-important parts of the map are printed in a lighter shade, while all the information for using public transportation is in boldface.

No matter where a person goes or what their **occupation**, it seems there are almost an unlimited number of maps to be used for work, play, or travel. As new technology is introduced, it is likely that new kinds of maps will be developed.

Chapter 4

Maps of the Future

Hundreds of years ago, relatively few people had need of maps. Most were not educated enough to read them, and very few people ever traveled more than a few miles from home. Today, world travel has become a possibility for more and more people. Even those who don't travel have a desire to know about the world they live in. The need for maps of all kinds continues to grow.

Cartography in the 21st century has become a mixture of science, art, and technology. Computers make it possible to construct three-dimensional maps that can be seen from different angles and distances. Plans and aerial photographs can be scanned and turned into computer information to create digital images for many uses. While surveying is still necessary, most of it is now done using airplanes and satellites.

Using GIS Databases

Satellite technology continues to improve as satellites allow us to see smaller and smaller areas

Computers have made it possible to construct three-dimensional maps like this one of Venus being viewed by a scientist.

more clearly. Satellites as a type of remote sensing allow a constant stream of new information to be entered into GIS databases. Satellites of the future will have many uses. For cartographers, they will continue to be a source of geographic information as the amount and types of information they gather continues to grow.

Because GIS databases are always being expanded, their use makes creating new types of maps both accurate and efficient. The uses for these GIS-generated maps range from government to business to public information. GIS technology can be applied to areas such as real estate, public health, crime mapping, national defense, the location and management of natural resources, transportation, and various individual uses.

Even though GIS technology allows mapmakers to make better maps, it requires much training to analyze data and understand the results. Because of this, GIS use is often limited to professional cartographers or other fields of science that use maps. Mapmaking in the 21st century is moving toward individual use as GIS companies look for ways to make GIS technology available to everyone.

Geocoding

One way GIS is helping individuals is through a process called geocoding. Geocoding creates personal-use maps for Web-based map programs such as Mapquest, Mapblast, Google Earth, and others. These Web-mapping programs are helping customers quickly find the nearest restaurants and other places they want to go. In the future, these programs may make it possible for customers to pick and choose which types of information they want to see and then create their own custom-made maps.

Maps of the future will not only be more available to individual users, but they will also include movement, sound, and multimedia effects. Those who create these maps will be able to view them from above, below, and from all sides. They will be able to change the size and scale at the touch of a button. Much like a virtual game of today, a traveler will be able to visit a new location without ever leaving his or her chair.

The maps of the future may also be able to respond to questions asked by the mapmaker. The response, in the form of a map, could give information about what might happen if a certain event took place. For example, someone buying or building a home would find it very helpful to have a map showing the effects of a severe flood, IF it were to happen.

Global Positioning Systems

In the late 20th century, a technology related to maps, Global Positioning Systems (GPS), was

Global positioning systems, or GPS, are now found in many brands of cars and make it possible for people to locate places without the use of paper maps.

developed using GIS information. GPS was created by the military for finding exact locations of missile launchers and other targets of military interest. In the 1980s, GPS technology was expanded for use in surveying work. By the turn of the 21st century, GPS had become available to the general public for personal use.

GPS is a network of 24 satellites that transmit information to hand-held receivers. The data transmitted by the satellites provides information about the longitude, latitude, and elevation of specific places or things. The receivers are tiny computers able to process data and store maps along with other useful information.

Travelers with mapping GPS receivers are able to calculate distances and directions to specific places. Some are hand-held devices, while others are now found in many brands of cars. Although not foolproof, these types of GPS devices are still being developed and will be able to provide more-accurate information in the future.

Geocaching

One use of GPS technology, called geocaching, is becoming a popular sport worldwide. Geocaching is a type of modern-day treasure hunting. Players use GPS **coordinates** to locate "treasures" hidden by others playing the same game. A treasure might be a souvenir from the home of a treasure hunter or a small item of some value, such as a baseball card. A player who finds the treasure makes a record of his find on a log page usually kept on the game's Web site. He then leaves something new for the next person to find. Some people make a vacation of traveling all over the world looking for these hidden treasures.

USGS National Land Cover Dataset

Wherever travelers go, having a map is always a good idea. Computer gadgets and GPS devices are helpful, but batteries do not last forever. To make sure that good maps are available to the public, the U.S. government established the United States Geological Survey (USGS). Their job is to oversee the creation of many types of maps. One such map is the National Land Cover Dataset. This collection of digital maps is available on the Web and as a CD-ROM. Future projects by the USGS will allow it to be updated from time to time.

Where Maps Will Go From Here

Thanks to satellite and modern mapping technology, most of the Earth has already been mapped. This does not mean, however, there is nothing left to map. Even though much is known about the ocean floor, there are still places to be explored. The deepest parts of the ocean are found in the Mariana Trench off the coast of Asia. In some places, the water is so deep scientists are still developing ways to explore it.

Another mapping opportunity of the future will be the Internet. Scientists, police, and others are looking for better ways to track the path of

Space probes like the Mars Odyssey are used to map solar systems and other planets in space.

communications over the Web. In this way, they will be able to find those who use the Internet for illegal purposes.

Space may well prove to be the final unexplored territory to be mapped. Although the job has already begun, there is still much work to do. Space probes and other spacecraft have been gathering information to be used in mapping since the late 1970s. Scientists are still analyzing much of this data. As future probes send back additional information, better maps of our solar system and its planets will be created. Someday it may be possible to take a vacation in space using these maps.

Whatever the future holds, maps in one form or another will continue to be part of man's travel, exploration, and study. Mapmaking methods may change, but man's need for them will not.

cardinal directions: The four main directions on a compass: north, south, east, and west.

cartographer: A person who creates maps.

cartography: The art of mapmaking.

circumference: Distance around the Earth at the equator; the edge of any circle.

coordinates: A system of using numbers and lines to find a point on a map.

cylindrical projection: A map made by projecting the features of a globe onto a cylinder wrapped around the globe at the equator.

geographical feature: Features of the land, including rivers, lakes, mountains, valleys, etc.

geologic formation: A feature of the land that can be mapped, especially rock formations.

latitude: Distance north or south of the equator measured in degrees.

longitude: Distance east or west of the prime meridian in Greenwich, England, measured in degrees.

map key: Tells what the symbols or colors on a map mean.

Mid-Atlantic Ridge: A chain of mountains on the floor of the Atlantic Ocean believed to be caused by the slow crunching together of two continental plates.

occupation: The job a person does to earn a living.

plate tectonics: The idea that the Earth is made up of large slabs of the crust moving against each other to create mountains and allow continents to float on the Earth's mantle.

population density: The number of people living in a given area.

precipitation: Water that falls from the sky in the form of rain, sleet, snow, or hail.

projection: A representation of a two-dimensional curved surface, such as the Earth, on a flat piece of paper.

scale: The relationship between the actual size of something and the size of a model or drawing on a map.

survey: To find measurements, position, boundaries, or elevation of an area of land by measuring angles and distances.

topographical: A type of map drawn to show the features of the land.

Books

Susan Julio, *Great Map Mysteries: 18 Stories and Maps to Build Geography and Map Skills*. New York: Scholastic, 1999. A fun way to put map skills to work and possibly learn a few new ones along the way.

Tish Rabe, *There's a Map on My Lap (Cat in the Hat Learning Series)*. New York: Random House Books for Young Readers, 2002. This one is just for fun but covers an amazing amount of information in rhyme.

Barbara Taylor, *Maps and Mapping*. New York: Kingfisher Publications (Houghton Mifflin), 2002. A basic how-to of map use with related activities.

Gertrude Chandler Warner, *The Mystery of the Pirate's Map (Boxcar Children Mystery #70)*. Morton Grove, Illinois: Albert Whitman and Company, 1999. In this timeless series about the Alden family, the kids find a long-lost piece of a map that could lead to a pirate's treasure.

Periodicals

***Which Way USA*—Highlights**—Illustrated maps and puzzle books from *Highlights* allow kids to use facts from the state maps to solve puzzles, find hidden pictures, navigate mazes, and meet famous people from each state.

Visit **highlights.com** or write Which Way USA, P.O. Box 10547, Des Moines, IA 50347-0547

Web Sites

maps-gps-info.com A Web site maintained by an individual who answers questions and is generally very helpful. No ads or pressure to buy anything.

scholastic.com/play/prestates.htm Interactive puzzle of the United States.

math.rice.edu/~lanius/pres/map/ Mathematics of Cartography contains information about how maps are made as well as activities and career possibilities.

yourchildlearns.com/megmaps.htm Free maps to print, ranging from one page to seven feet across in size. World and U.S. maps available.

Index

Aerial photography, 13–14
Ancient Greek maps, 7–9
Angle measurements, 12
Atlas, first, 9

Babylonian clay tablets, 5–6

Cardinal directions, 6
Cartography
    computer technology for, 19–21
    early, 9
    future of, 32–40
    in Middle Ages, 9
    nineteenth century, 11–12
    during Renaissance, 10–11
    twentieth century, 13–21
Chinese maps, 7
Circumference, 8
City maps, 29–31
Clark, William, 11
Clay tablets, Babylonian, 5–6
Columbus, Christopher, 7
Compasses, 12
Computer technology
    Geographic Information
        System (GIS), 19–21, 32–34
    Global Positioning Systems
        (GPS), 35–37
Contour lines, 23–24
Cylindrical projection, 11

Dark Ages. *See* Middle Ages
Digital maps, 38

Earth
    circumference of, 8
    crust of, 16, 27
Egyptian maps, 6
Elevation, 23–24
Engineers, 26
Eratosthenes, 7–8

Geocaching, 37
Geocoding, 34–35
Geographic Information System
    (GIS), 19–21, 32–34
Geographical features, 22
Geological maps, 26
GIS databases, 32–34
Global Positioning Systems
    (GPS), 35–37
Google Earth, 35
Greek maps, 7–9
Grid lines, 9

Han Dynasty, 7
Highway maps, 29
Hydrologists, 26

Infrared light, 17
Internet, 38, 40
Iraq, 6

Landsat satellites, 19
Latitude, 9
Lewis, Meriwether, 11
Light spectrum, 17
Longitude, 9

Map key, 22
Mapblast, 35
Mapmaking. *See* Cartography
Mapquest, 35
Maps
    ancient Greek, 7–9
    Babylonian, 5–6
    Chinese, 7
    city, 29–31
    digital, 38
    early, 4–9
    Egyptian, 6
    geological, 26
    GIS-generated, 19–21, 32–34

Picture Credits

About the Author

Wendy Lanier is an author, teacher, and speaker who lives in Beaumont, Texas. She is married to a college professor and is mother to two daughters and three dogs. The dogs are way more trouble.